STANISLAS
TOMMASINI
(1827–1913)

MISSIONARY TO THE AMERICAS

Caroline Richard

Stanislas Tommasini 1827–1913
Missionary to the Americas

Cover illustration: Portrait photo anonymous.
Book design by Peggy Nehmen, n-kcreative.com

Printed in the United States of America
ISBN: 979-8-9946784-2-8 (paperback)

Published by:

4120 Forest Park Avenue
St. Louis Missouri 63108-2809
314-652-1500
www.rscj.org

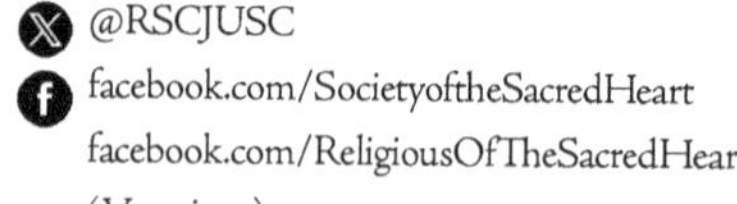

CONTENTS

Introduction v

1.   Young Marietta 1

2.   Introduction to the Society 3

3.   Finding her Footing...7

4.   Revolution 13

5.   Across the Atlantic 17

6.   Travel Companions... 21

7.   Back to Havana 27

8.   *Annus Admirabilis*... 33

9.   Guiding Novices in Canada and Coteau 37

10.   A Covert Mission 43

11.   Life in Mexico... 49

12.   Final years... 55

13.   Conclusion 59

Chronology 65

INTRODUCTION

The Society's General Chapter of 2024 decided on a geographical reconfiguration of the provinces in the Society. The RSCJ in the United States – Canada Province learned that they would be joined with those in Mexico and Puerto Rico in a new province to be called ANAM. Preparations began to become acquainted with one another's language and culture. The USC Province Publication Committee reflected on how it could contribute practically to this project. In the past several years, we had produced brief biographies of some of our founding mothers to introduce them to new Associates or partners in mission. We decided to have these translated into Spanish to make them available to our Spanish-speaking sisters and their constituencies. The use of DeepL facilitated and speeded up the translation. Short biographies of Saint Madeleine Sophie and Saint Philippine, originally written in English, have now appeared in Spanish.

In addition, we decided that some of those RSCJ responsible for the establishment of the Society's foundations in the various countries should be better known throughout the new province. Carolyn Osiek, RSCJ, therefore revised an earlier biography of Mother Aloysia Hardey written by Ruth Cunningham, RSCJ, which was also translated into Spanish, and we commissioned Caroline Richard, the director of Le Petit Musée at Grand Coteau, to write a contemporary account of the life of Mother Stanislas Tommasini, who had worked in all four countries of the new province and who might be considered its patron. As she had left a memoir behind, her biographer had a primary source at her disposal. Caroline has made excellent use of it in presenting this attractive, holy religious of the Sacred Heart.

1.

YOUNG MARIETTA

Maria Luigia Angelica Cipriana Stanislas Tommasini exuded joy in every corner of the world where her life in the Society of the Sacred Heart took her. Her passion, her zeal, and her deep sincerity won the hearts and souls of all she touched. From modest beginnings in 1827 in the Italian duchy of Parma, Stanislas Tommasini was the youngest of three daughters, born to loving, hard-working parents. Marietta, as her family called her, was a cheerful child, full of happiness and movement and love.

In her memoirs, she described her mother as a saint, her sisters as angels, and herself as an *enfant terrible*. Throughout her life, she recounted stories of her mistakes and transgressions. A serious and devout Catholic, her mother Angelina was forever correcting her youngest daughter for displays of vanity, outbursts of song, and distractions during prayers. She found she could not help herself. She had inherited her father's fondness for flowers and music and beautiful things. Young Marietta loved all kinds of music, and her singing voice was a particular vanity. She recalls, as a five-year-old, sitting in her garden singing to herself when a local noblewoman heard her. The woman stopped to listen, greatly praised her talent, and told her she would be a singer one day. Marietta's mother became so worried by this comment that she forbade her daughter to sing anything but the Litanies of the Blessed Virgin Mary. Another day, while alone in a room of her house, Marietta heard music coming from the street outside her window. Completely swept up in the melody, she began to waltz around the room using a chair as her dance partner. Her mother, who strictly forbade dancing, caught her in this act of frivolity and put her to work for the rest of the day.

Like many young girls, Marietta argued with her mother about wearing the most fashionable clothing and shoes. Concerned with indulging her daughter's physical vanity, her mother had forbidden Marietta to curl her hair. One day, knowing her mother would be absent for a stretch of time, Marietta sat in front of a mirror and got to work. She managed to form three perfect ringlets before her mother returned, discovered what her daughter was doing, and quietly walked up to her with scissors and cut off the three curls completely. Marietta described the reproach as humiliating but very effective.

While her two older sisters were obedient and virtuous and a great comfort to their parents, Marietta kept her mother and father on their toes. Her father would tell her stories of the saints, hoping to inspire her to imitate them. She admitted that the lives of the saints did not appeal to her; rather she wished to be like the angels she saw around the church, blowing her trumpet loudly.

2.

INTRODUCTION TO THE SOCIETY

In 1834, when Marietta was seven years old, the Society of the Sacred Heart founded a convent in Parma. Annette, the middle Tommasini daughter, expressed an interest in religious life, and a priest introduced her to the Religious of the Sacred Heart. Mother Lavauden,[1] the superior in Parma, encouraged her to stay home for a year to study dressmaking before her entrance. Throughout that year, Annette and her sisters were invited to attend weekly Mass at the convent. Marietta remembers picking figs with the religious, walking through the gardens, and singing with the children at the free school. While her life at home was characterized by austerity and simplicity, the religious encouraged her playfulness, gave her books she greatly enjoyed, and suggested her father take her to concerts. For the first time, Marietta began to understand that happiness and holiness can exist at the same time.

Soon, an important visitor came to the convent, coinciding with a heartbreaking event for Marietta. In 1842, traveling from Rome, Madeleine Sophie Barat visited the house in Parma.

---

1 Angélique Lavauden, born 1787 in Grenoble, entered in 1809, was professed in 1813, and was one of the founders in Turin 1823, Parma 1843, and Perugia. She died in Montfleury, France, in 1872.

Marietta recalled seeing her walk the convent grounds from the windows of her house, and even had the honor to meet her. Mother Barat spoke with Signora Tommasini, embraced her, and told Marietta she was blessed to have such a holy mother. At the same time, Marietta's sister Annette, then an aspirant, was sick with tuberculosis. Sophie allowed her mother to stay with Annette to take care of her overnight in the convent and keep her comfortable during her illness. Marietta watched her older sister become weaker and more infirm, yet hopeful and thankful that she would enter heaven as a Religious of the Sacred Heart. Before her death, she bequeathed her vocation to Marietta.

In the months following, Marietta spent more time with the religious. She began to take her sister's bestowal to heart and to realize the depth of her own vocation. Her oldest sister, Rosina, had also entered the Society and was a novice at the time. When Marietta brought up the subject of her own admission with Mother de Lahoussaye[2] one day, she was told it was her duty to stay home and take care of her parents. Likewise, when she approached her own mother with her petition to join the Society, her mother laughed at the idea, not believing her daughter took the commitment to religious life with any seriousness. After a long discussion, however, her mother began to see that this was not an empty request, and cried tears of joy. Her father's response: "This is the first sorrow you have caused me! Go if God calls you, and take my blessing."

Like many religious orders at the time, the Society had a two-tiered system of membership. Marietta assumed she would be

---

2 Julienne Rosalie de Lahoussaye, born in 1799 at Quimper, entered in 1824 and was professed in 1833. She was part of the foundation of Lille, and wanted to go to America, but instead was sent to Parma, where she was beloved for her generous service during ten years. Later, she served in Genoa and Chambéry, and died at Montfleury in 1854.

admitted as a coadjutrix sister, the religious responsible for domestic duties, and would take her sister's place as seamstress. However, after seeing her aptitude and ability, the superior admitted her as a choir religious, one of the mothers who served in teaching and leadership roles.

3.

FINDING HER FOOTING

As the Society was making plans for a new foundation in Padua, Marietta was named among those to be sent there. On November 21, 1843, a group of fourteen religious left Parma for the four-day journey to Padua. This was the first time she had been outside of her province, and she relished every moment of the new adventure: riding in the coach, seeing unfamiliar countryside, and listening to her fellow religious tell stories of their travels. She was especially moved, as they stopped in small villages to change mules, to hear the mothers converse with local women and children, talking to them of the love of God. She was struck by the kindness of Mother de Limminghe[3] who always gave her fellow travelers more food than she allotted herself and who gave Marietta a rosary belonging to Mother Barat when she realized she had misplaced her own.

The travelers arrived in Padua to take ownership and operation of an existing boarding school. Marietta tried to settle into life as a postulant, but found herself in trouble just as often as when she

---

3 Louise de Limminghe, RSCJ (1792-1874) was born in Belgium and entered the Society in Ghent in 1813. She was superior at Turin, Padua, and Genoa, assistant general in 1839, and mistress of novices in Rome. She was a close friend of St. Madeleine Sophie and an important witness in the cause of her beatification.

lived with her parents at home. When given the task of sweeping an empty music room, she was found seated at the piano singing litanies instead. Unconsciously she sang as she completed her chores, too often at inappropriate volumes. Once, a bishop, seated in the parlor, heard her singing in rooms far away and asked her superior who was singing so loudly. Her clumsiness was also a constant source of disapproval. She broke items as she dusted or dishes as she washed; sometimes she would bring a stack of broken dishes to her superior because she had not had the courage to show anyone at the moment of the accident. Despite these setbacks, Marietta was not discouraged; she remembered her sister's dying request and continued to strive to be worthy. When she asked permission to begin a novena to St. Anthony to help find the spirit of the order within her, her superior suggested she first make it through nine days without breaking anything. She had to restart five times.

Around this time, Mother Anna du Rousier[4] was named vicar, a kind of regional superior, and made a visit to Padua. In a private interview, she and young Tommasini discussed at length her talents and her virtues, as well as her struggles and shortcomings. Mother du Rousier decided to have Marietta accompany her to Turin, stopping in Parma to visit her parents. There, she received her parents' blessing and was again reminded to be humble and to be obedient. Her mother left her with the words, "Be friends with all, but confide in only one: this Mother Superior who holds the place of God." After traveling together with her, Mother du Rousier kindly called Marietta to her and told her that she was

---

4 Anna du Rousier, RSCJ (1806-1880) was professed in 1831. After serving in Padua and Paris, in 1851 she was named visitor of the fifteen houses in North America. From there, she assembled a group to found the Society in Chile in 1853, where she remained for the rest of her life.

as yet too childish, and that much reflection, calmness, and maturity were needed before she could receive the habit. She would go to the house in Saluzzo for a year to work on these things.

Mother Anna du Rousier

In Saluzzo, in a small community with only twenty students, Marietta studied, read works of literature, and prepared vestments and candles for Mass as under-sacristan. She soaked in the wisdom of the religious around her. After a year, Mother du Rousier brought young Tommasini to Pignerolo, another foundation in northern Italy; there she continued her studies, practiced humility, and began to gain confidence as a leader among the students. She did her best to temper her enthusiastic outbursts, allowing what she called her "good angel" to rein her in. A small event at Pignerolo would have a lasting impact on the young postulant. A Jesuit priest from Mexico visited the convent and recounted the story of Our Lady of Guadalupe to the community. Tommasini was immediately enchanted with his description of the beauty of Mexico and the moving story of the Blessed Mother appearing to a poor man in the countryside. A lifelong love for Our Lady of Guadalupe was ignited.

Tommasini continued to work hard. Those around her helped to spiritualize her love of beautiful things, to find God in the beauty of music, poetry, and nature. After some time, she wrote to Mother du Rousier asking permission to quietly assist in the sacristy during an approaching retreat for the religious at Pignerolo. Her answer granted more than she had hoped for: she would be allowed to attend the retreat entirely and she would also receive the habit. Upon this news, she began to dance, sing, and jump about. When told to contain herself, Tommasini replied, "Oh, Mother, I've been containing my joy for a year. I cannot do it any longer."

Tommasini returned to Turin to join the novitiate there. Despite the growth and maturity she had achieved over time, Tommasini felt she was starting over, struggling with expectations of her. Again, she battled her pride concerning her singing voice and committed numerous mistakes as she taught classes, gave exams, polished floors, washed dishes, and performed various other tasks around the convent. Once, during the novena for the feast of St. Stanislas, the novices were each assigned a holy hour in the chapel. When Tommasini's hour approached, she accidentally made her way to the wrong chapel, found herself locked inside, and spent the night there alone until someone found her in the morning. Her time in the novitiate was filled with many lessons in humility such as this, yet she never doubted nor did she forget the impact of the deep love and affection Mother du Rousier felt for each of her novices.

More than once during this time, Tommasini was told she was unready and still had much to learn before she could make her first vows. Toward the end of 1847, afraid that her vows would be delayed, she wrote a letter to Our Lady of Guadalupe asking for assistance and placed it under a statue of Mary. A few months later, Tommasini's prayers were answered. She was admitted to the celebration of her first vows.

At her next destination, the house of Soccorso, she continued to learn and work and receive guidance along with the other young religious there. Her superior, Mother Thérèse du Lac,[5] spoke to them of incidents happening across Europe and of the dangers threatening the Society of the Sacred Heart. She told them stories of Philippine Duchesne and the missionary work being done by the Society in America. It was clear that Mother du Lac was gently preparing Tommasini and the other young women for events on the horizon.

---

5 Marie-Thérèse du Lac, born in Piedmont in 1817, entered in Pignerolo in 1837. Professed at Turin in 1845, she later served in Chile, 1854-1865, and in Spain, where she died in Seville in 1875.

4.

REVOLUTION

The next years were ones of turbulence for Tommasini's beloved Italy. She spoke of these times with sadness for the closing of convents and the upheaval of her fellow religious, yet with gratitude that it contributed to the Society's expansion into the Americas. The spirit of revolution had been spreading across Europe, reaching the Italian provinces by the 1830s and 1840s. Uprisings were taking place in various regions, with revolutionaries calling for reforms, new constitutions, and the overthrow of oppressive regimes. When Pope Pius IX opposed the attempted overthrow of Austrian rule in the northern provinces, anti-Catholic sentiment among reformers spread.

One evening in March 1848, revolutionaries planned an attack on the Jesuit houses in Piedmont; to many of the posted notices was added the phrase: "Tomorrow the Sacred Heart!" That night, not knowing what to expect, the religious brought all of the students into the community area, the room located farthest from the windows that opened to the street. An organ was brought in and the children were allowed an impromptu party, dancing and singing in an attempt to block out the noise from the demonstrations outside. When the pupils were finally put to bed at a very late hour, the superior told the religious to remain dressed and alert in case the situation escalated. The community watched in prayer. Near one o'clock in the morning, rioting crowds arrived in the streets outside the convent. Despite having closed and shuttered doors and windows, they could hear the revolutionary cries calling for the death of the Jesuits and the death of the Religious of the Sacred Heart. Thankfully the crowds moved on without incident and not a single child awoke. During trying times in her own leadership roles later on, Tommasini would remember the heavy responsibility placed on her superiors as well as their bravery and trust in God on that night.

In the coming days and weeks, the Jesuits were expelled and Sacred Heart houses across northern Italy found themselves in increasing danger. They were accused of corresponding with exiled priests, holding unpatriotic meetings, and lying about what they were teaching the students. A revolutionary disguised in a stolen habit was found in one of the convent kitchens, attempting to uncover incriminating evidence. In some houses, students were sent home and religious forced to conceal themselves in lay clothing and flee to other convents. The communities in each of the houses were told to put their affairs in order, arrange all necessary documents, destroy what could be considered dangerous, and be ready to leave at a moment's notice.

Tommasini's own time to flee was soon at hand. Following a series of harassing letters, protestors climbed the chapel walls, shouting insults into the convent windows. She would join a group of about ten Religious of the Sacred Heart, undercover in ordinary clothing, as they fled to Chambéry in France. It was a cold and treacherous journey through the Alps, stopping occasionally to warm up, change mules, and listen for any news of what lay behind or ahead of them. When the group arrived safely in France and was dispatched to various houses there, Tommasini found herself relocated to the Rue de Varenne, at the time the motherhouse in Paris.

Hotel Biron, rue de Varenne, Paris, where Tommasini arrived after expulsion from Piedmont, 1848.

After so much fear and unpredictability, she was comforted to be in the presence of her blessed superior general again. She was able to meet with Sophie Barat. They talked of Tommasini's sisters and parents and of the house in Parma where they had first spoken; she told Sophie that it had been her wish to join the missions and go to America after hearing Mother Duchesne's letters. Tommasini was struck by the intensity with which Sophie listened, allowing her emotions to show as they spoke. She remarked that Sophie marvelously combined the qualities of mother and superior. It was there that Tommasini found that she was bound for America, to Mother Aloysia Hardey[6] in New York.

6 Mary Ann Aloysia Hardey, RSCJ (1809-1886), born in Maryland, moved with her

As preparations got underway for the voyage to America, Sophie called Tommasini to see her again. She delivered the sad news that the house in Parma had been closed and all the religious relocated. They talked of the mothers who had guided and taught her there; Tommasini confided that they had found her childish. Sophie smiled and told her to be a child all her life, but be a good one. Tommasini would eventually come to understand the difference between childish and child-like.

family to Louisiana, where she was one of the first students at Grand Coteau and entered there in 1825. One of the founders of St. Michael, professed there in 1833, she was superior there, in New York, and was responsible for foundations in Canada and Cuba, before becoming assistant general in Paris.

5.

ACROSS THE ATLANTIC

In the summer of 1848, Sophie gathered the missionaries together, blessed them, gave their final instructions, and sent six Religious of the Sacred Heart to board the *Noemi*, a merchant vessel bound for America. On the ship, Tommasini embraced the spirit of adventure, reveling in details of life at sea, from the adjustments to their daily spiritual exercises to the stories told by the other passengers. However, as the weeks wore on and the excitement of the voyage wore off, each of the travelers was thankful to finally reach the port of New York. The young postulant who met them at the door of Manhattanville was unnerved by this group of women who spoke no English and wore shabby travel clothes, but Mother Hardey was prepared for their arrival. She had religious clothing laid out and the chapel ready for their prayers of thanks. Following these stressful months of uncertainty and upheaval, Tommasini would remain the next twenty-three years of her life at Manhattanville and develop a deep and lasting friendship with Aloysia Hardey.

Tommasini spent her first year at Manhattanville working in the novitiate, in awe of Mother Marie Thérèse Trincano[7] and her

---

7 Marie-Thérèse Trincano was born in Milan in 1809 but raised in Switzerland. She

instruction and guidance of the novices. Mother Trincano had spent her own noviceship in France under the earliest mothers, and Tommasini became increasingly aware of the importance of this continuity. Sometime after her arrival, Mother Hardey called

Aloysia Hardey, superior at Manhattanville

Tommasini to her office to inform her that Sophie wished her to learn Spanish. Manhattanville's chaplain, Father Goldecano,[8] an exiled priest from Venezuela, was to teach her. Tommasini grew anxious at this prospect as she was eager to learn English instead.

---

entered at Besançon and was professed in Kientzheim in 1837. She came to America in 1847, and became the most trusted helper to Aloysia Hardey. She was the first superior vicar of Canada, 1864-1868, and died at the Sault in 1868.

8 Efforts in connection with an earlier publication have been fruitless in identifying Father Goldecano.

She expressed her concerns that Father Goldecano knew only English and Spanish, while she knew only French and Italian. How would the arrangement work? Mother Hardey countered, "It doesn't matter; obedience will find a way to make it happen."

Life at Manhattanville was simple and strenuous, but happy. The school had little money to hire help, so the religious did all the housework. Tommasini enjoyed teaching the young students games and Italian songs, but shed many tears of frustration at not being able to communicate well in English. The children, unable

Manhattanville convent

to understand her instructions, would simply ignore her directives. Over time however, her English improved. In addition to her duties in the convent, Tommasini taught catechism to local Italian immigrants, and despite her initial reticence, she took much pleasure in her Spanish lessons. A quick learner, Tommasini welcomed new literature to read in Spanish and listened to Father Goldecano recount stories of revolution in South America and religious persecutions similar to the ones she had fled in Italy.

In 1850, the first students from Mexico arrived at Manhattanville. Rafaela and Adela Nuñez, sent to New York for shelter from some of the political unrest unfolding in Mexico, were placed in the care of Mother Tommasini. She was to teach them catechism and see to their needs in the boarding school. Rafaela especially remembered the special care taken of them, and she would later play an important role in the Society's coming to Mexico.

Tommasini came to know yet another exile during her time at Manhattanville. One day, a Spanish gentleman and father of three Manhattanville pupils came to the convent with news that a Mexican bishop, Monsignor Pelagio Labastida, had arrived in New York, recently exiled from his diocese in Puebla. Mother Hardey wasted no time inviting him to the convent, settling him in a residence on the grounds, and providing English lessons with Mother Tommasini. The two grew close, and upon leaving New York sometime later, he told Tommasini, "You will be one of the foundresses of the Sacred Heart in Mexico."

6

TRAVEL COMPANIONS

One of the happiest positions Tommasini held in all her years as a Religious of the Sacred Heart was that of traveling companion of Aloysia Hardey. She was often asked to accompany her superior as she visited other houses in the region. In her memoirs, Tommasini describes one particular trip in 1852 from Manhattanville to the day school on West 17th Street. Because of unfriendly sentiments toward Catholics in New York, the religious usually wore secular dress when they traveled between the houses. On this particular trip, Tommasini gave into her vanity and made an attempt to wear fashionable clothing. She raided the play closet and found a gray silk dress with the largest hoop skirt she could find, which she wore over her religious habit. Despite a disapproving look from Mother Hardey, the two began their trip downtown. The heavy silk dress and heat of the day did not mix well, and Tommasini could not reach her handkerchief to relieve her sweat. In addition, the large weighty bag she carried pushed heavily on the hoop skirt, causing it to fly up in the back. As they boarded the omnibus, Tommasini realized the size of the skirt kept her from being able to sit. At one point, she fell backward into a seat on the bus, and the hoop skirt sprang up revealing her habit under the dress. She was mortified! When they arrived at the day school, Mother Hardey turned to her coldly saying, "I never want to see you in this costume again." Tommasini was thoroughly ashamed and assumed Mother Hardey would never forgive this offense. Many years later, however, after a retreat at the motherhouse, Mother Hardey recounted the story to all the superiors, adding to Tommasini, "You never knew how much you amused me!"

Tommasini often made the trip to 17th Street with Mother Hardey, both in secular clothes, either by omnibus or the wagon of a tradesman. Tommasini, with her natural curiosity and enthusiasm, attempted to ask questions or comment on the scenery; Mother Hardey opted instead for silence or her rosary. In May 1854, Tommasini made her final profession in the chapel of Manhattanville, and that summer she was chosen to accompany Aloysia Hardey to visit the house in Halifax, Nova Scotia. Tommasini was to pass for her maid on the journey, and she played the part with great distinction, entertaining Hardey with her interactions with fellow travelers.

It would not take long for Tommasini's Spanish lessons to be of use outside of New York. For years, families and clergy in Cuba had been petitioning the Society of the Sacred Heart to come to the island. Many Cuban girls attended Manhattanville, and some entered the Society afterward. The superior of the Jesuits in Cuba often wrote to Mother Barat asking her to establish a house there, but fear of yellow fever and uncertainty of funds made her wary of proceeding. However, when Anna du Rousier took the Society to Chile in 1853, there was further incentive to settle in Cuba to create a stopping point on the voyage from New York to Santiago. Finally in 1857, Sophie granted Aloysia Hardey permission to travel to Cuba to assess the situation firsthand; Tommasini would accompany her as interpreter. Mother Hardey, Tommasini, and two other religious set sail on the *Cahoba* and arrived in Havana to a grand reception. The Espino family, a Cuban family eager for a school for their daughter, had prepared generous accommodations and met them at the port in a large and elaborate boat. Despite their wish to attend Mass in quiet anonymity, the religious were escorted in highly decorated carriages and placed front and center in the church, after first being presented with a large number of expensive gifts. The public spectacle of their arrival and welcome to Havana, however, proved to create difficulty for the travelers. Despite assurances from the Archbishop of New York that the Society was most welcome and that all Cubans awaited their arrival, there were political divisions facing the island. Loyalty to Spain versus growing sentiments of independence, a recent economic crisis leaving financial uncertainty, and increasing calls for the abolition of slavery were all factors in play. Mother Hardey in particular, as an American, was viewed as an obstacle by those who opposed United States influence in Cuba. In consideration of all these factors, Cubans were wary of upsetting the balance, and no one was coming forth with resources or plans to secure a foundation for the Society.

Tommasini watched as Aloysia Hardey made her next moves. After setting aside some days to assess the situation in her mind, reflect on various factors, and pray for clarity and guidance, she requested an audience with the Captain General. As Tommasini interpreted, Mother Hardey expressed her gratitude for their warm welcome, but found that Havana was not quite ready for a foundation at the moment. Without a suitable location for a school and the funds to establish it, she would be returning to New York shortly. Faced with this eventuality, the Captain General quickly jumped into action, located several possible sites, and raised a large sum of money for purchase. Mother Hardey wrote to Manhattanville that a property had been secured and they were ready for reinforcements.

Tommasini observed Mother Hardey's skillful methods as they prepared the house. At one point, Tommasini wished to write to the United States for cheaper materials and tools and more dependable laborers. Mother Hardey told her it was always better to work with local merchants and materials, even at your own expense, in order to earn the goodwill of the people. She taught Tommasini the importance of belonging to the city and serving its people, rather than remaining outsiders.

As preparations continued in Havana, Aloysia suffered a sudden attack and was taken very ill. It was just as Sophie had feared: yellow fever. For several days, Tommasini remained at Hardey's side as she suffered. She called doctors at all hours of the night, administered their treatments, and most importantly, prayed. People came from all corners to assist. Enriqueta Purroy, a friend in Havana, provided and insisted on an application of almond oil. Rafaela Donoso, a young woman requesting to enter the Society, offered to spend three extra days in purgatory in exchange for a cure. After a week hovering between life and death, Hardey seemed to turn the corner toward recovery. When Tommasini declared that prayer had saved her, the doctor replied, "Ah, you religious never want to give credit to the poor doctor!" During this anxious and worrying time, Tommasini began to see the people of Havana in a new light. She was struck by their extreme kindness and generosity. Masses were offered across the city, funds raised for the poor, and prayers extended, all in the name of Mother

Hardey's recovery. Tommasini admitted that she began to know and love the inhabitants of Havana in a special way in the course of that trip, remarking in her memoirs, "I have always noticed that the more we know people, the more we love them; the love kindled in my heart by so many acts of charity has never cooled."

Mother Hardey's recovery was full, and the school opened its doors on the nineteenth of March 1858. Mothers Hardey and Tommasini returned to Manhattanville shortly afterward.

7.

BACK TO HAVANA

This eventful stay in Cuba was hardly the last time Tommasini would visit the island. In 1867, Aloysia Hardey was called back to Havana, again with Tommasini as interpreter, to settle some business issues. As before, political divisions were impeding the operation of the house there. The recently appointed bishop of Havana, Jacinto María Martínez y Saez, was resistant to a foreign congregation's operating in the city, especially one that took orders from an American superior; and he was making life increasingly difficult. He had taken away some of their privileges in the city and dismissed their only confessor who spoke multiple languages, a hardship on the members of the community who were not fluent in Spanish. On their visit to Cuba, the bishop refused to meet with Hardey, and she and Tommasini were forced to return to New York having accomplished nothing. It was clear that there were larger issues at play: the bishop saw himself in a power struggle with the Captain General; he did not believe he was receiving the amount of respect due him, and he resented the Society's international connections. When Hardey and Tommasini returned to Havana the next year, they did so with a new tactic: humbling themselves at the feet of the bishop.

The two were finally awarded an audience. Upon entrance, Hardey and Tommasini fell to their knees and remained there for over an hour. The bishop laid out his grievances with the Society; Hardey kissed his feet and humbly begged forgiveness, but the meeting ended only with his rather cold blessing. In her memoirs, Tommasini recounts the story of the boat ride that followed this meeting. Traveling to another foundation in Cuba, the religious found themselves aboard the same boat as both the bishop and the Captain General. Trying to remain inconspicuous, but too curious as to what was happening around them, Tommasini lifted her veil at just the same time the bishop looked over, and she was recognized. They were forced to beg a second audience with the bishop, which thankfully mended their relationship somewhat further. Hardey and Tommasini were able to return to New York having made progress.

One day back at Manhattanville in 1870, Tommasini was called to Mother Hardey and told to go into the city and apply for her passport: she was to be superior in Havana. Tommasini fell to the floor, feelings of surprise, fear, and doubt running through her head. She questioned her ability to be superior; she feared leaving her home of Manhattanville, and she loathed the idea of leaving her beloved Mother Hardey. She did her best to prepare for her departure, tried to recall comforting words of Madeleine Sophie, but remained in shock. As the time to sail approached, Tommasini was called to the parlor where she found Mother Hardey weeping. The thought of leaving her dear Reverend Mother without her steady companion of the last twenty-three years now opened Tommasini's own floodgates. The two stood together unable to speak, until Hardey finally said: "Let us be faithful wherever God sends us, advancing step by step toward him, desiring, hoping, believing that he wants all that happens to us. Let us live in such a way as to lead souls to good through love for the Sacred Heart. Let us fulfill our duties with simplicity, gentleness, patience, help for the weak, sympathy with the suffering, and trying to smooth the rough paths. The life of a superior is a life of constant effort, of persevering self-denial, a word to this one, a look to that one, a show of intelligent and effective interest in the affairs of each. The life of a superior must be all goodness, all affection, and this joyfully." And with that, Tommasini set sail.

Having been to Havana many times already, Tommasini was well-suited to understand the needs of the foundation there. She made some physical changes, adding ventilation in some areas of the house to make the heat and humidity more bearable, as well as some changes to the spiritual life of the house. While the bishop had restored many of their privileges, the French and American sisters were still without a confessor who spoke their language. To assist them, Tommasini created books for each. Pages were divided into two columns with some relevant phrases in French or English opposite the Spanish; she offered her own services for specific translations. Things progressed smoothly in her first assignment as superior. She praised the spirit within the house, crediting Mother Hardey with having laid the initial groundwork for the religious there, and extolled the generosity of their Cuban families donating so much time and money to those in need.

One evening in 1872, two years into her superiorship, Tommasini sat with her community during recreation. With no advance notice, Mother Hardey walked into the room causing Tommasini to burst into tears of joy and kneel at her feet. Hardey confided that she had been called to Paris to be assistant general and had chosen Havana to begin her tour of the North American houses.

Although neither spoke of it, Tommasini knew the sadness in her heart to leave all of her American daughters. The visit, however, was full of joy. After her illness and recovery from yellow fever, the families in Havana claimed Aloysia Hardey as one of their own and gave her a happy sendoff.

El Cerro, first house in Havana.

Translation: Front of the building of the
Colegio del Sdo Corazón del Cerro Havana

El Cerro back patio.

Patio de los pozos del Convento del Sdo. Corazón del Cerro

Translation: Courtyard of the wells of the Convent of the Sacred Heart del Cerro.

8.

ANNUS ADMIRABILIS

The next years were a whirlwind of countries, cities, and positions for Tommasini. In 1873, only three years after becoming superior in Havana, she developed an acute pain she could not ignore. When her doctor found a tumor and insisted on surgery, a cable from the Motherhouse ordered her back to New York for the operation. Her doctors, wishing to delay the surgery during the unusually hot summer, advised sending Tommasini north to Halifax with plans to operate in the fall. However, when she returned to New York in October, the doctors could find no trace of her cancer and canceled the operation. Tommasini attributed her recovery entirely to Madeleine Sophie.[9]

Her doctors would not allow her return to Cuba, and so Tommasini became superior at 17th Street in New York. Her stay there was cheerful but short. In 1874, Aloysia Hardey returned to New York to tour the North American houses again and deliver news from the new superior general, Mother Adèle Lehon.[10] She

---

9 Madeleine Sophie Barat had died in 1865 and was already being invoked for spiritual and physical favors.

10 Adèle Lehon, RSCJ, superior general 1874-1894, had previously been for many years superior in Rome at Santa Rufina and then at the Villa Lante.

was met at the ship by her former travel companion, and as so many times in years past, Hardey and Tommasini drove together uptown to Manhattanville, in happy silence as ever before. There Tommasini received her new post: vicar of Canada. Once again, she lamented this new responsibility, questioning her capabilities and dreading her new task of deciding vocations. As before, she was told to trust in the Holy Spirit and all would be well.

Tommasini would call her next year, 1875, her *Annus Admirabilis*. Not long after she set to work in Canada, she was summoned to Paris by Mother Lehon to discuss important affairs. Her response, that she was eager to go but could not possibly get away at the moment, was met with the directive to leave at once. Mother Lehon would later tease her for postponing an order from her superior general. Mother Lehon sent Tommasini to visit various houses in France and Italy in an effort to excite interest for the missions. On this tour, the truly international nature of the Society was apparent to her. While abroad, she visited with Canadian women about to enter the novitiate in France. She happened upon two Mexican sisters who had attended Manhattanville, yet she knew them from her time as superior in Cuba. And all of these women were connected by their love of the Sacred Heart of Jesus. While she was at the house at Conflans outside of Paris, Mother Lehon invited Tommasini to accompany her to meet the Holy Father, Pope Pius IX, in Rome. On the way, they would stop in Parma to visit her own dear mother. Tommasini was overcome.

As they traveled, Tommasini noted how much easier and safer travel between Chambéry and Turin now was. Instead of a mule-driven cart over the Alps, she was now comfortably aboard a railroad carriage traveling through tunnels. What had not changed, however, were the generous warm exchanges among her fellow sisters as they traveled. When the group arrived in Turin, Tommasini continued on to visit her aged mother in Parma. She entered the house and ran straight to her mother's bed as her mother cried, "*Marietta, piccola bambina.*" It was a beautiful reunion as the two talked about the joy the Society had brought her and the extreme happiness of loving God.

Moving through Italy, she garnered generous donations for her missions in Canada, met former pupils and their own children, and saw religious she had not met since her early days in the Italian convents. Tommasini's time in Rome was beyond her expectations. She visited an endless number of churches and shrines, including the chapel of her patron, St. Stanislaus. As she listened to church bells and looked out at rooftops and steeples from her windows, she was taken by the beautiful and holy atmosphere of the city. Adding to her bliss, she was allowed to make a retreat in the same room in which Madeleine Sophie had stayed at the Trinità dei Monti. Of the retreat she exclaimed, "I saw clearly my own nothingness and even more clearly that God is everything; I understood in a striking and ineffable way what it means to have Jesus for a companion."

As if her travels were not already beyond her expectations, Tommasini was invited to accompany Mother Lehon to her audiences with Pope Pius IX. She listened as the two talked of the 1871 Paris Commune and revolutionaries at the convent doors. The pope discussed the increased devotion to the Sacred Heart throughout France, and the Society presented many gifts to the Vatican to be distributed to various missions. Tommasini was introduced as coming from America, but the pope was quick to recognize that she was from Italy. During their second audience, Tommasini made the childlike gesture of kissing the pope's robe and silently placing her rosary in his hand as he conversed with the superior general. The pope smiled and said, "She is still very Italian," to which Mother Lehon graciously responded, "I would not wish her otherwise."

With their day of departure finally arrived, Tommasini reflected on the beauty and awe of the time she had spent travelling across Europe, spending joyful hours visiting holy people and places. She felt prayer was not adequate to express her happiness, so she began to sing, adding her own lyrics to the hymn of St. Francis: "Praise be to you, my beloved Lord, for this wonderful year 1875 placed so admirably in the wicked life of Tommasini." Her *Annus Admirabilis* concluded with one final gift, a long visit with her beloved Mother Hardey in Paris before setting sail.

9.

GUIDING NOVICES IN CANADA AND COTEAU

Stanislas Tommasini returned to Canada, her spiritual life replenished, gifts for her Canadian houses in hand, having left behind a deep fervor for the American missions. One of the religious told her there would be no postulants left for Europe if she stayed much longer. Tommasini spent seven years as vicar of Canada, a time she described as seven years of happiness living a sweet family life with good friends to support them. In her memoirs, she mentions students, friends, alumnae, and numerous local clergy who contributed to this sense of intimacy in Canada. Their kindness and generosity led to the growth of both the academy and the free school in Montreal. Tommasini recounts times when she would go to the chapel, in despair over lack of money, only to return to her office to find an envelope in the day's mail containing the exact amount of funding of which she was in need.

When Tommasini first arrived at the Sault-au-Récollet, the Canadian novices had been recently relocated to Kenwood Convent in Albany, New York. Bishop Ignatius Bourget, a great friend to the Society in Montreal, expressed his regrets to the superior general that young Canadian aspirants had to leave their country for formation. He received a promise from France that the novitiate would reopen at the Sault once there were enough Canadian postulants to justify its return. Tommasini considered herself privileged to be on hand when this promise was fulfilled and novices arrived back at the Sault on the day of the Assumption in 1876. She felt deep love and a great responsibility to form these young souls, so full of zeal, in the spirit of the Society.

Sault-au-Récollet, 1856

Having had the great fortune to know personally so many of the early mothers of the Society of the Sacred Heart, including Madeleine Sophie, Tommasini understood the importance of imparting their spirit to young religious. She sang and taught her novices the old hymns she had learned in Italy and France. She spoke with such love and sincerity of the Society, recounting words of advice she had received from Sophie, Aloysia Hardey, and many others, conscious of how much they had helped her in the past. Tommasini's own struggles with maturity, humility, and obedience allowed her to be all the more sympathetic to her novices struggling with the same. She was patient and respectful in her guidance. One of her former novices said of her sympathy, "If the task imposed on our developing virtue seemed heavy, we felt understood, we knew that our mother had gone through similar trials."

In 1881, Tommasini was sent to look after a new family of novices, those in Grand Coteau, Louisiana. Likening herself to the Magi following the star, she recounts, "Finally my star stood over Grand Coteau. At the primitive station called 'Sunset,' I was faced with a carriage worthy of the poverty of Mother Duchesne." She recalled the rustic charm as well as the deep religious spirit that pervaded the house; she was particularly touched to be in the house where Philippine Duchesne stayed, near the well from which she drew water, and to pray in the chapel in which Mother Hardey had made her first communion. The enthusiasm and joy that characterized Tommasini to everyone she met were especially appreciated during her time in Grand Coteau. The novitiate journal describes countless congés and a surprise wake-up call at four a.m. so they would not miss viewing a comet. When a young professed raced down a flight of stairs and almost crashed into her superior, Tommasini admonished, "What of the rules of modesty?" The young religious fell to her knees recognizing her fault, but Tommasini followed with, "I am old and I still run. What can I reproach this youth with? My daughter, I was worse than you."

Tommasini was superior of the house as well as mistress of the unique trilingual novitiate there. Grand Coteau had long been home to both English- and French-speaking novices; but in 1874, when Havana joined vicariates with Louisiana, the novitiate began to include Spanish-speaking novices from Cuba, and later Puerto Rico and Mexico.[11] Tommasini had to repeat her instructions in three languages to ensure she was understood by all. A former novice described this process in which spiritual reading was read first in French by a Spanish-speaker, then in Spanish by a French- or English-speaker, with evening prayers recited by a Spanish-speaker. She explained that all this served as a means of formation. Father Montillot, S.J., the rector of St. Charles College in Grand Coteau, studied Spanish in order to hear the confessions of the Spanish-speaking novices as well as provide instruction.

Born and raised in Italy, fluent in four languages, having spent time now in France, the United States, Cuba, and Canada, Tommasini not only epitomized the international nature of the Society of the Sacred Heart, but communicated its significance to her young religious. Just as she left Canada for Grand Coteau, the Canadian novices sent two letters to the Grand Coteau novices, one in French, one in English. The novitiate journal records, "Our Mother Tommasini, in coming here, has united our novitiate with theirs in an inseparable way. How true it is that the sacrifices which cause some separations only strengthen this dear Society." She was remarkable in building community among diverse groups, appreciating their multiple nationalities while uniting them within the

---

11 Before Tommasini arrived at the international novitiate in Grand Coteau in 1881, most of the Spanish-speaking novices were from Cuba. The foundation was made in Puerto Rico in 1880; and the first Puerto Rican novice from the new foundation, Isabel Salazar, entered the Grand Coteau novitiate in April 1881 under Tommasini's direction. Isabel made her first vows in August 1883 in Santurce, Puerto Rico. Tommasini had already left Grand Coteau for the foundation in Mexico in April that year. Later, in 1893, Tommasini, as superior, welcomed Isabel to the day school in Havana as econome. Isabel's vow crucifix with her initials etched on the back is in the Puerto Rican archives in St. Louis, Missouri.

Three Puerto Ricans had entered the Society before the foundation in Puerto Rico. Two were at Grand Coteau before Tommasini arrived, Josefina Marín having entered in 1877 and Rita Rivera in 1878. Catalina Mojarrieta had entered at Kenwood in 1868.

Cor Unum. And after only two years in Louisiana, Tommasini's international travels would continue.

Grand Coteau novices with Tommasini (second row)
and Victoria Martínez, 1881–1883

10.

A COVERT MISSION

If Tommasini followed her star to Grand Coteau, it would appear as if all her stars aligned in her next mission. From her early devotion to Our Lady of Guadalupe to Sophie's decision for her to learn Spanish to her numerous interactions with Mexican students and clergy during her time in Havana and New York, Tommasini seemed to be destined for the call to Mexico. For years, the Society had received requests to send Religious of the Sacred Heart to that country; for years, the superior general remained wary. As the convents in France and Italy had recently survived revolutionary movements unfolding around them, the Society was not eager to place religious in a region that was dealing with similar tendencies.

As early as 1810, as Mexico began to throw off the Spanish Bourbon monarchy, it also began a social revolution targeting Spanish aristocrats. Catholic Church officials generally fell in line with the crown and belonged to this aristocratic class. The situation remained unstable for many years, one side seizing power from the other and European and American forces exerting their own interests. In 1857, a series of reforms began, affecting the influence of the Church in Mexico. These measures included the seizure of church land by the government, the secularization of education, and the dissolution of religious orders. These laws of reform, while ushering in some necessary changes, also took religion away from many Mexicans whose lives had been centered around the Church for generations. The measures resulted in many aristocratic families sending their daughters to Society schools in the U.S. and Europe, and led to the exile of Bishop Labastida, who—as we have seen—would befriend Tommasini at Manhattanville.

While Tommasini was guiding young religious in Montreal and in Grand Coteau, forces were working to encourage the Society to come to Mexico. Cousins Rafaela and Adela Nuñez, the young students from Mexico whom Tommasini had taught and watched over at Manhattanville, were continually writing to Aloysia Hardey for a Sacred Heart school. They were active, building churches, helping priests, attempting to gain favor with government officials, and spreading the word to prospective families. Some influential individuals, whose daughters had also attended Manhattanville, renewed their petitions for a school and promised to help pave the way. In the 1870s, Bishop Labastida, who had once predicted that Tommasini would be a founder of the Sacred Heart in Mexico, was allowed to return to Mexico City.

In 1882, Superior General Adèle Lehon wrote to Mother Elizabeth Moran, vicar of Louisiana and the Antilles,[12] of this increased interest in a foundation in Mexico. She talked of

---

12 Mary Elizabeth Moran, RSCJ (1836-1905), born in New Orleans, entered the Society in 1853. After many years at Grand Coteau, she was named superior vicar of the houses in Louisiana and Cuba. She was thus part of the foundation group to Puerto Rico in 1880 and to Mexico in 1883. She was then named superior vicar of Spain in 1895, but was recalled to France three years later. She died in Belgium, one of the exiles from the French expulsion.

Tommasini's enthusiasm and zeal, but worried about the restrictions imposed on religious orders there. Even if they were able to operate their school, they would have to avoid all exterior religious

Bishop Pelagio Antonio de Labastida y Dávalos (1816-1891).

signs, including wearing the habit. The following year, Tommasini was summoned to Mother Moran in New Orleans. Mother Moran had been given permission to take a group to Mexico to investigate the situation firsthand; the religious would have to operate with secrecy and discretion, careful to remain anonymous. Tommasini would accompany as translator. She described her joy as she ran to the chapel, "God alone could understand a soul at this moment. All I could say to Him was: 'Finally, finally!' It seemed as if I could suffocate from joy." Her first order of business was to write to Labastida, who was now Archbishop of Mexico City. When no answer came, they considered delaying departure, but instead pressed on, fearing an imminent yellow fever quarantine that would delay them for months. Mothers Elizabeth Moran, Kate O'Reilly, and Tommasini donned their secular dress and left the port of New Orleans on April 14, 1883. As luck would have it, their secret mission was at once in jeopardy. Despite traveling in disguise, Mother Moran was recognized by a former student and word spread throughout the passengers, one of whom was an official in the anti-Catholic government. Not knowing what their next steps would be, the religious disembarked at Vera Cruz and prayed that the Heart of Jesus would guide them. Miraculously, two women in a small boat arrived and told them, "We have been sent by the Archbishop, do not let anyone know who you are." They were given a place to sleep for the night and the next day left for Mexico City where they would be in the hands of Amanda Andrade, another alumna eager for a Mexican foundation. Tommasini describes the picturesque scenery from the train as they traveled: majestic mountains, green valleys, and vast plains. At their first stop, Orizaba, she marveled at the imposing volcano in the distance, at the clothing and customs of the people, in disbelief that she was finally in the country of Our Lady of Guadalupe.

With Miss Andrade's help, they were brought to Bishop Labastida; he explained the sensitivity of the situation and apologized he was not able to show his outward signs of welcome. He informed them that President Manuel González knew of their arrival in Mexico and they must take care; enemies were watching them and looking for any excuse to expel them from the country. They were beginning to see the extent of the task ahead of them; even the Jesuit priests they were acquainted with pretended not to know them. But with prayer and patience, things progressed. Former students from Manhattanville began to find them; prospective parents came to them promising their daughters; all the while, the religious sidestepped attempts of government officials to find them out. They searched in secret for a suitable convent, relying on friends to guide them. They were told of an eccentric older woman with a possible location for a school and were invited to her home to discuss. When they arrived at what they thought would be a private dinner with allies, they were surprised to find a formal gala, surrounded by government officials and other important people, many hoping to find proof that the women were indeed nuns. Tommasini quickly assessed the situation and decided at once she would approach the guests without fear. She worked the crowd as cheerfully and comfortably as any lady there; and by the end of the evening, she had the partygoers not only convinced that they were not religious sisters, but questioning why they had ever thought so. Their enemies, somewhat less threatened by their presence, eased up surveillance, and after about three months in Mexico, a convent location was secured.

11.

LIFE IN MEXICO

Just as Bishop Labastida had predicted, Mother Tommasini was indeed one of the founders of the Sacred Heart in Mexico. When the convent received its first students on August 1, 1883, Tommasini greeted them as superior, mistress general, and mistress of class; enrollment reached 100 within a month. As always, her cheer and joy reigned. She filled any position in need of assistance, seeing no job beneath her. If a student recreation was perhaps lacking in enthusiasm, she would appear like lightning: singing, dancing, animating the children, then disappearing just as quickly.

Despite a merry familial atmosphere within the school, criticism and suspicion of the religious still remained without. Newspaper critics often published damaging stories, painting them as American women coming to get rich at the expense of Mexico. President González had declared they would be expelled if he could be sure they indeed belonged to the Society of the Sacred Heart. Authorities often showed up at the convent unannounced to inspect the building. When this happened, the religious would throw on secular clothing, hide all the children in one classroom, and calmly escort the official through the building.

In many cases, the performance was merely a pretense. Once, an authority whose own daughters attended the boarding school arrived to inspect the house. After his inspection, he whispered

First school in Mexico, 1883.

to the superior that he would return the next day as a private citizen to visit his daughters and chat with her. Tommasini found the situation laughable. Finally, an official who had inspected the house several times before arrived at the door to find Mother Tommasini, fully dressed in her religious habit. She told him, "You see, General, I wear my uniform just as you wear yours." He stammered back, "Nothing is more appropriate." The days of disguises were over.

In 1884, Porfirio Díaz became president, ushering in an era of industry, railroad, and development. As Mexico rose on the international scene, it became more desirable for government officials to send their daughters to Society schools. Even Díaz's own daughter attended and his wife belonged to the Children of Mary.

Three years after opening the first house, the number of Religious of the Sacred Heart in Mexico grew from fourteen to fifty-three, with many Mexican women joining the novitiate located in Grand Coteau. In 1887, Mother Tommasini was called to be superior at the house in Guanajuato, founded almost two years earlier. Once again, she rose to the occasion, performing every task with eagerness and zeal. The children at this house generally came from families with extravagant means, and she made it her mission to instill the humility and simplicity she herself had been taught. She was especially proud of her students when they chose to remain at school during the Christmas Novena rather than attend their families' luxurious parties. She eventually won over even her enemy, the former president, Manuel González. González, who had once sworn to expose and expel the Religious of the Sacred Heart, was now the governor of Guanajuato. Upon hearing he was suffering from a serious illness, Tommasini wrote him a long heartfelt letter and enclosed a Sacred Heart medal. Her words must have touched him, because he responded with his personal thanks and an offer that she must send word to him should she ever need his assistance.

The Society continued its expansion in Mexico and opened a house in Guadalajara in 1895; Tommasini arrived there after some weeks to become superior. Also in 1895, Elizabeth Moran, who had been vicar of the Antilles and Mexico for some time, was called to Europe. Under Moran's leadership, the Mexican houses were characterized by a freedom of spirit and warmth and adaptation. Jeanne de Lavigerie,[13] a Frenchwoman brought up

---

13 Jeanne de Lavigerie, born in Bordeaux in 1851, entered at Conflans in 1876 and was professed in Paris in 1884. She was superior vicar of Mexico and Antilles, 1895-1902, then assistant general. She died in Rome in 1932.

under Mother Mabel Digby and faithful to the strict observance of cloister and the rule, took her place. The houses in Mexico tended

Mary Elizabeth Moran, RSCJ.

to follow some of the local customs; clergy entered the convent parlor freely and enjoyed greater access to the religious than was the case according to Society rules. Mother de Lavigerie felt it her duty to bring the houses back to observance of the Society's customs and made changes to curtail some of these practices. The locals, especially in Guadalajara, did not appreciate this shift. The public scorned and criticized them, accusing the religious of pride and arrogance, even extending those accusations to those outside the convent, for example, to the Children of Mary. At the age of sixty-eight, Tommasini struggled with the situation unfolding.

She received a small respite from these stressful times in 1897 when she was invited to travel to New York for the Golden Jubilee of Manhattanville. The trip took her first through New Orleans, where the younger religious gathered around her to listen to her discuss her favorite topics, her love of the Society and the beauty and goodness of God. When she arrived at Manhattanville, she felt the absence of Aloysia Hardey, but was quite moved to be back in her old home and received with such love. On her return to Mexico, she made a stop in Grand Coteau to visit her old friend Father Montillot for the last time. He celebrated Mass for her in the chapel there and gifted her with a poem before she continued on her way.

Her joyful trip down memory lane visiting old friends and former homes was punctuated with sadness on her return to Mexico. She received news of the death of Mother Kate O'Reilly in Havana and was called back to Cuba. After thirteen years in her beloved Mexico, Tommasini was leaving for the last time. She would be dearly missed. Letters and notes from families and former students poured in praising her dedication to the souls of not only her pupils but of their families as well. Her beautiful, ardent singing voice, her devotion to Mary, and as always her fervor and passion for the work of the Society would be remembered. Rafaela Nuñez extolled her big heart that was capable of winning over so many other hearts. The lives of those she touched in Mexico were forever grateful.

12.

FINAL YEARS

Under normal circumstances, it would have been a happy reunion for Tommasini returning to Havana and the community there. Not long after her arrival, however, in April 1898, Spain and the United States declared war on each other, and Cuba found itself in the middle of the conflict. The day after the declaration of war, boarding school students left the dormitories and returned to their homes. As fighting reached the island, many local families requested shelter; Tommasini housed people in need around the grounds of the convent. The blockade of the island led to a shortage of food and supplies, and the Children of Mary in Havana organized a great deal of aid for the groups suffering the most. The religious did their best to keep going; Tommasini kept morale strong with encouraging words, her cheerful nature, and constant prayer. After running out of bread, she told her community that they would always be rich as long as the Lord was with them. The *Annual Letters* during this time express their consolation that although they experienced a shortage of resources, they never felt a shortage of spiritual assistance. Though short in duration, the conflict took its toll on the community; the *Annual Letters* record the deaths of four sisters over those months.

In October 1899, Tommasini announced she was bound once again for Grand Coteau. The community in Grand Coteau, especially the novices, were thrilled to have their former mother return. While her time there was meant to serve as a well-deserved rest after her difficult stretch in Havana, it was clear that Tommasini was incapable of slowing down. She offered to teach classes, assist other instructors, and arrange Christmas preparations to the last detail. From Grand Coteau, she returned to Manhattanville where, again, she made herself useful. She taught French classes, worked with the sodalities, and helped the children put on elaborate plays. She was named assistant of the day school and, as always, served as a voice of guidance to the younger religious, offering advice that harkened back to the founding mothers. In 1904, she celebrated fifty years of profession alongside Mother Sarah Jones, the vicar, another religious from the early days in New York. Religious of the Sacred Heart and Manhattanville alumnae poured in for the festivities, expressing their gratitude and veneration for these women and their many decades of work and dedication.

During these early years of the new century, the religious in America anxiously followed events in France. A progression of secularization laws posed the question of whether the Society could remain in that country; all the French religious were sent to other countries. For Tommasini, it recalled the days of her own exile, the closing of Italian convents, and the suffering endured by many. The situation, however, brought her one great consolation. In 1905, the closing of the convent at Conflans made necessary the relocation of the religious buried there, including Aloysia Hardey. With immense gratitude and warmth, Tommasini was allowed to attend a Requiem Mass for her dear Mother Hardey at Kenwood Convent in Albany, New York, where her body would be laid to rest.

The following year, she herself moved to Kenwood. There she spent the rest of her days writing to her numerous children around the world and playing the role of a devoted grandmother to young religious, including some of her Mexican pupils who were delighted by the reunion. In 1910, she was invited to Manhattanville to prepare the students for a reception for an Italian cardinal. She taught the children to sing a beautiful Italian chorus and to read the address so well that the cardinal told the students he felt as if he were home in Italy. In her final years at Kenwood, Tommasini could be found in prayer, in service, and more often than not, in song. The community could hear her singing throughout the house, often teaching students and novices the old hymns of her youth.

September 15, 1913, was a day spent like most of her days. She reminisced about her life in Mexico; she was overheard singing in her room; she spent the evening at recreation talking with the novices and delighting them with stories and advice; she gave a kind word to her secretary and retired to her room for supper. She was found there, not long after, unconscious and partially paralyzed. She revived, but over the following days, the community witnessed her health declining and her paralysis increasing. As she took her final breaths, the community rejoiced in her happiness at a life well-lived, full of passion and zeal in the Heart of Jesus. She was laid to rest at Kenwood, on the left side of Mother Aloysia Hardey's grave.

13

CONCLUSION

The international nature of the Society of the Sacred Heart calls for a certain amount of cultural appreciation, understanding, and adaptability from its members. This is where Stanislas Tommasini shone. She transcended nationality, belonging only to God, the Society, and her daughters. At the same time, she seamlessly adopted and fell in love with the customs, traditions, and people of every country and house in which she lived. Sensing the ever-increasing expansion of the Society across the world, Sophie recognized Tommasini's natural curiosity and her gift of connection and channeled them to beautiful ends. In her lifetime, Tommasini served the Society in four languages across six countries.

Tommasini spent the most formative years of her religious upbringing in the presence of the early mothers of the Society, including Madeleine Sophie herself. She received formidable words of encouragement and advice from these mothers, and she, in turn, imparted them to each new generation of novices she instructed. This allowed for a continuity of leadership style and tradition within the convents as they stretched across continents. She treasured her relationships with the likes of Anna du Rousier, Aloysia Hardey, Sarah Jones, and Elizabeth Moran and understood the value and necessary effort of making sure their stories and insights remained alive. Young religious sought out her direction, taking in her simple, yet captivating wisdom. Every time she assumed a new position, she made a point to praise and value the person she was replacing and honor what she had accomplished.

Throughout her life, Tommasini lamented her struggles with humility and obedience. She always somehow saw herself as the childish creature not quite ready to receive the habit. Never discouraged, Tommasini used every admonition or correction as a tool to improve her character and therefore better serve her beloved Society. These efforts served as their own method of formation; her own struggles and faults helped her novices realize they too could overcome theirs. At the age of 78 when she traveled to Puerto Rico with Mother Mahony,[14] the sisters there were struck by her humility and her ability to be of great use while simultaneously fading into the background to allow others to receive praise. Young Marietta Tommasini would be pleased to see her older self's absence of pride.

While Tommasini herself remembered mainly her faults, others remembered simply her joy. Her tendency to break into song at any moment continued well into her old age. Once, a younger sister came upon her singing an Italian song and playing castanets beside a statue of Mary and an arrangement of flowers. Mother Tommasini told her she was simply having a little feast with Our Lady. She never lost the childlike nature Madeleine

---

14 Ellen Mahony was born in St. John, New Brunswick, in 1843. She entered in New York in 1861 and was professed in Paris in 1870. Called "Dean of Vicars," she was Superior Vicar of Canada, 1881-1888; of the West, 1888-1892; of New York, 1895-1908; and again of Canada, 1908-1925. She died at the Sault in 1925.

Sophie saw in her. Her sense of playfulness had a wide range; she enjoyed jumping rope with the young children just as much as assuming undercover roles to avoid government officials. Her spirit was irrepressible and her enthusiasm seemed to have no bounds. Every ounce of her energy and passion was poured into expressing her love of God and of the Society of the Sacred Heart. On the day in 1845 she received the habit, Mother Anna Boriglione told her, "May you never lose the atmosphere of this day of peace and happiness." Tommasini swore she never did.

Scapular worn by Madeleine Sophie and Stanislas Tommasini.

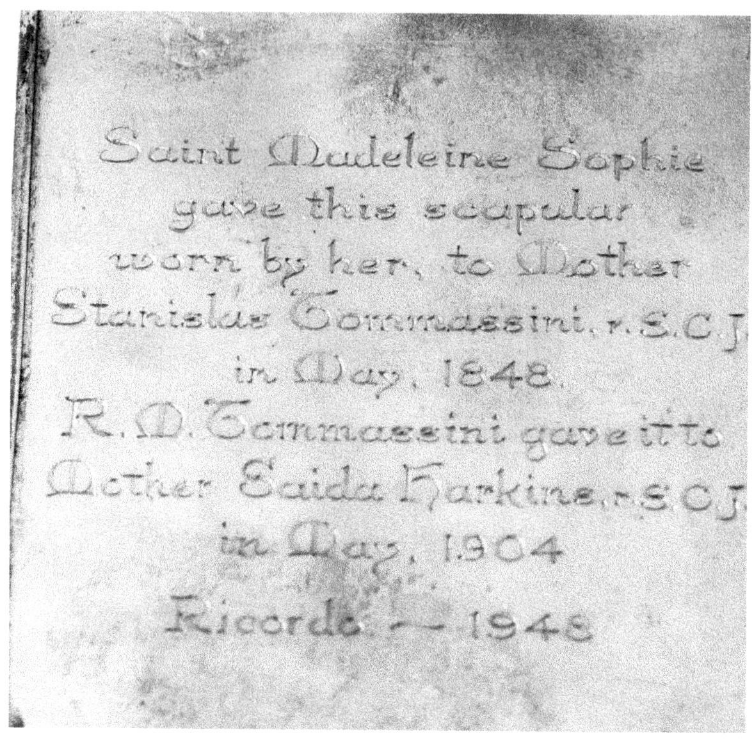

Scapular inscription on the back of the case:
"Saint Madeleine Sophie gave this scapular worn by her,
to Mother Stanislas Tommasini, RSCJ, in May 1848.
R. M. Tommasini gave it to Mother Saida Harkins, RSCJ,
in May 1904. Ricordo 1948."

Grave of Stanislas Tommasini in Kenwood Cemetery,
next to that of Mother Hardey.
Photo: Lynne Lieux, RSCJ

CHRONOLOGY

1827 – Birth of Maria Stanislas Tommasini in Padua, Italy

1843 – Entrance into the Society of the Sacred Heart

1848 – First vows, expulsion from Italy, voyage to New York, arrival at Manhattanville

1857 – Travel with Aloysia Hardey for foundation in Cuba

1870 – Superior in Havana

1873 – Superior at 17th Street New York

1874 – Superior Vicar of Canada in Montreal

1881 – Superior and mistress of novices in Grand Coteau

1883 – Foundation of Mexico: superior, mistress general, mistress of class in Mexico City; superior at Guanajuato and Guadalajara

1898 – Superior in Havana

1899 – Grand Coteau

1900 – Manhattanville

1901 – Assistant Superior and French teacher at New York day school

1906 – Retirement to Kenwood

1913 – Death and burial at Kenwood

* 9 7 9 8 9 9 9 4 6 7 8 4 2 8 *